SPACE ODES

SPACE ODES
R. T. A. PARKER

BOILER HOUSE PRESS

ODE AT THE END OF THE WORLD 3
THE BOX 6
THAT BALL 8
MENDING WALL 11
ODE ON EMPATHY 12
JOHN LEWIS 23
KUMAR SANGAKKARA 24
DÖNER 33
HEADINGLEY CLINAMEN 35
ALL THE BLEAK CHIPPIES 39
ROOFS 41
POCAHONTAS 43
LAURA BRANIGAN 44
WORK IN SPACE 50
TWO PATHS 56
THE A1 57
ODE TO DOGS 65
BRING UP BETHLEHEM 66
ODE AT THE BEGINNING OF THE UNIVERSE 69

SPACE ODES

for my father

ODE AT THE END OF THE WORLD

It's the Wild West
and on the ridge the rancher-robot
    sports among the antelope,
the desalination plant whirring.

It's 5am so I get up and set the rotors running,
wipe down the outhouse.

It's 5am and I'm up tending the square,
while on the western ridge the antelope sport.

I'm a rancher-robot wending its way westward,
where the buffalo play
and the mountain lion atumble with the gazelle.

I apply the medium roller.
The servos pull and the outhouse bustles on its moorings,
    shifting against the rising breeze.

On the other horizon the comms. bank,
but the radio is dead.
And the light green grass
only a thin layer on the dust.
Tails flash across the prairie,
a squirrel turns to listen.

So, at the end of time, I tended the generators,
the moisture farm.
At the end of time kept the square cropped and ready.

It's the Wild West,
and all our life, the maintenance droids,
weren't we just trying—
>   trying finally to apologise with the right intensity
>   for ever having been switched on.

On the dunes, the antelope.

For a gecko the desert's not so bad
(licks own eye). It's not so bad here
for the albino buffalo.
No, nor not so bad for the deadwood dirtpan first eleven—
prairie below, the prairie sky above
baked dirt, the lone autoroller.
Keep the square square though the world has ended,
though brute fascism walked the land and the world ended.

It's the Wild West, and all the antelope sing:
"I think we are the only person who is always there."
Once again the antelope sing:
"Is the world of the antelope of the prairie and of the world?"
Don't know,
               antelope.

It's the morning, sun rising
and the vaparators aren't going to fix themselves.

At lunchtime I'm the antelope,
rolling, righting myself while I flick my ears
for footfall, distant shootout, thunder in the noonday sun:

>   brothers and sisters
>   we're all broken robots. We're
>   iterations imperfect as the pines of the forest;
>   wonky copies rooted, dumbly worried;

> the grizzly giants of the Wild West;
> the withered bristlecones of the clear High Rockies;
> the schools of carrier bags turning
> > round the oceans 'great green whirlpools.

As the sun nears its apex
it's the Wild West,
let's rebuild the universe.

A thousand years since the world passed,
but three bags still swirl,
the old reactors tick in their concrete skirtings.
The robots fix the machines
in the split-apart blown world.
Where / how will you find a song of community?
In the birds?
In the grass-rustle?
> —A song to welcome the dawn
> and the International Brigades'
> "march on ghost feet"? At the branch-creek
a world so tart and untouched
the wilderness-cyborg senses the sublime;
"rewire the machines, the multigrade sunset."
"Empty world!" cry the squadrons of aquadrones
up and down the banks of the unquiet ocean;
further west the waves
and the deadening grey of the spray and the droplets like veins zip
   off the visor.

Sex in the world was an ordeal.
Just a little further to the homing beacon.

THE BOX

What you scatter's mostly the box,
your eye—it casts about and wham
I'm yours, or my box.

Yes, and that same day
I started a poem about death
this one guy died. You expect
it, but one guy I knew, you know?

*

& thus to you, nameless, I write
this the death ode; this the chalk eye
that swings as you're just past and safe,
that tilts—your straight back, unturning.

What! Like John Paul Jones you thought
you cleared the hedge; though that none-seeing
from up and out the hedgerow rolls on,
apprising itself of your wide brim

& your velvets against the sky
like celluloid (explosive)
the spark off your half-dome shining
& a whole horse sweating under you.

& on, then. Man & eye. A trio. For one more
once more, bestilled, the cracked casement.
He's up there too, spacing out now
as when you for the first time stop

you let the heat the space soak in
to you and have a beer. And just.
Completely. Relax. Death stalks you.
You're him for that instant.

THAT BALL

The first vidicard: Friday the 4th of June 1993.
Marky Mark Wahlberg used his poo to grow up greens in the spare vegisphere
with, what, couscous or something for the sandy outfield
gritty loamy meatloaf, Pukka Pies for "the hallowed strip in the haze"
in the slips three drones;
    a ghostly android plays to the bowling of an android
    in the wide empty empire of space.

French cricket with the exoskeleton cargo-loader;
you're all androids with tagliatelle on your insides for tendons
the spinning boundary with the artificial gravity on,

the centre is everywhere
the circumference nowhere;

what I remember is:
    all the withering plants of the dying Earth
    all the greens lined long and straight in the hangars,
    barracks for animals, sleeping, the engines always throbbing

    and in another place all the dishes of Earth
    filed in cabinets—on rolling belts
    captured piping hot

they couldn't stop the warming
so the animals and the grass upped and left.
And I'm a cyborg with a re-engineered biological brain
so I don't need downtime
but I've got these other confusing memories
I have to sift through from the vidibanks

and we've got a game of French cricket in the great loading bay
five dimensional cricket in the clanging echo of the liquivat
　—twelfth man in a tabard, a fleeting glimpse at the rim
the last man—the only ghost upon the Valley Forge as the crickbots
　play.

At bat my mind whirrs and chirrups like fine machinery
but all of the rest of the time
I'm haunted by inaccessible pasts, others' pasts
goodness the past
　　but, on 111 or in the dicey 70s
from the edges of my visor
　　　the field is full of shades
—all life entropy
—the memory is empty, nothing.
Memories I couldn't have known
but we make them and they pierce us.

　*

October 1st 1993
igloos and Eskimos and penguins and ice
a hell of a place to be coming from
the strange simplicity of the past
in the cold Calgary air I'm not smoking I'm breathing
the sad music simpler because it's no longer real
the heat, the humidity
not Tiesto but Garrix, not Albinoni but Giazotto but Barber
but the fucking past, all of which
is true.
　　　　　Where / how / what nostos Diplo?
　　　　　What nostos Diplo?
　　　　　What is left?

And who knows which shadow coast we near
the scratch game on Goose Green or on Shell Green
our brave boys out for the dark side,
our spheres are biological matter, we shall deposit them
across the universe;   Ongar loam
Surrey mould
the shitsward headlong through interstellar space.

The hulks, the silent arks
         flicker to and fro,
nothing but blue skies,
chemtrails.

MENDING WALL

All else is quite clear,
   remaining so, the ontos the ice
   like deltas round the pressure holes
   all else is clear, remains so with the thaw
   as the late ice-mist a foot from the ground
   level with stile and dry rockfall,
   as if under the pressure of the unperceived
   the wall falls open
   like the bebeingness of the beasts
        that stalk the orchards at the blackening solstice;
   viscera outrageous, toothy whoopee cushions.
   And the creak of the loose end of the decking
   as at evening you crack the Appletini,
   wave off your open upon its piercing jet.

ODE ON EMPATHY

It's twenty to five in Wetherspoons in Black Heath; half eight in the Coliseum, a Wetherspoons in Abergavenny, on a Friday; lunchtime at Wetherspoons, The Kentish Drovers, in Peckham; it's a thousand years ago in The Royal Oak in Tunbridge Wells, in Petts Wood's The Daylight Inn thirty years ago, in the Old Blue Last, the Blue Posts and in the other Blue Posts it's six and a half years into the future; in all of these pubs it's half past seven at night, or just ticking through to eleven, or it's the early afternoon—particularly it's 14.30 in the Fox on the Hill, it's the Prince of Wales, the Sir Robert Peel; at 22:30 on a Sunday the earth shaking, it's all the times at once as we held each other, already ghosts; Forest Hill Wetherspoons during the attack, the blast rushing through; The Moon Under Water, it's 19:45 and the Champions League; Casa Paco's, the many similar xiringuitos of Catalunya, it's two thirty in the morning out on the tepid sand with two shooting stars—
    we're fixed just here in togetherness,
    in limitless boundedness,
    in exquisite collaboration
                            —or at the Lamb on Lamb's Conduit Street some other time; at the Oval at whatever time with whomever; under the McDonalds arches by Old Street round the back of Angel on Baker Street at the Westport in St. Andrews by St. James's Kingsland Road at various points (the Russian Bar, the Jazz Bar) Old El Paso on Old Street the Lumiere Barden's Boudoir the numberless scenes of orgy the chikhai bardo at some exact point in some exact place the Skyrack about a quarter to seven the Cricketers in Kennington at five past one the Cricketers at Newington Butts about quarter past one the Cricketers on Broomhill Common at twenty-five past two—

Many years from now,   the lithium deposit on Mars played
      out,
   the dispensary closed up,

     old miner kicking his heels, begins to feel vital,
          like a real thing materialising suddenly in the corporate
               Denkraum,
   feels this panic come over him
          and sets to work at the controls
      adrenalin, that growing anxiety;
     all those years he's been rolling around bored out of his mind,
          buzzing or crashing off the glucose rations, head skipping
               around
    would have just loved to feel something—
  But wheel him up to but the very edge
        the crust
  see the distant lights of the ring road, the clear far light of reality
               —*bring up the ore!*—
  and the old blood's pumping and he just wants out of it like limerence
          like Jesse Tate from *The Naked Spur*;
     remembers that it was awful;

              "never forget how terrible it is to fall in love."

You drink to try and feel things and also not to
     it's just to feel the states changing
but it never does / you never do
like the sandwich doesn't shift it,
              passes through, the microplastics and cancer.

Interested in being in between the different states,
constantly in motion
> [though we're always changing and between],
never drunk the same way twice
not sip the same cold lager (Herodotus);
> bright afternoon slipping into evening.

Try this for a tagline:
Ice cream: It Makes You Forget.
Or: Ice Cream: It Moves You Constantly Between Remembering and Forgetfulness;
Ice Cream: Linger in the Movement / At the Interstices.

*

It's Mars at a certain time and it's a certain time in the hills above the city, it's a particular time in what was once the dole office and it's a long lost time in all the old record stores and a far off future time in all your neat start-ups and an eternally moribund present in the pop-ups and it's now and forever the management meeting now the meeting when we'll discuss the monitoring mechanisms now the meeting during which we'll discuss the new desks and the seating plan and the chain of command the schools merging the faculties merging departments divided now the meeting to implement the module evaluation questionnaires the meeting to respond to the tyrannical VP or to the tyrannical student reps ["executive furies of the robot lord of death"] the virtual Freshers' fair at 17.00 while it's 16.20 and school's out or 18.00 and work's all done but then what just other times the edifice unbending so find something to do with your time find some way to freedom or is it facilitating your freedom in your leisure hours or more likely your recuperative hours your spare moments they drag behind you bring no respite all your anxious hours are a working.

For example:

I'm a long-suffering PI, excited and
walking quick around the city on Mars in the night
   ragged after the dopamine,
    the magic passing out of the world.

I'm drinking to extinguish social conditions—though I don't get far with it.
                               We're alone when we drink,
       sharp elbows at the bar.
  And we're steely as we choose, for love is injustice—society written through it like rock.

All the boozing is a contraction.

Drinking and reminiscing down the local in the afternoon,
        saw the last cartwheeling fragments of a spaceship
with the heat shields glowing
two other lovers who'd died a thousand years before
        aspark in the gloom.

Another couple across town,
a property developer closing a deal,
a ditherer at the precipice,
        all looking up and each sees it,
not knowing the others.

    And we're all finally the same and the clouds are coming,
glittering the interference field, we cross into the next stage:
    And then this one time I woke up and it was four in the afternoon
    and I'm getting dressed in front of the mirror,
    rolling round on the bed,
    then getting dressed again and repeatedly grabbing my neck.

In a funk because there's nothing to do in the afternoon.

Then it's the night and I'm off out
in, say, Manhattan the Meatpacking District
or Montmartre,
and I'm doing this weird offhand dance in some half-empty very
    lit-up disco
where it seems like I've gone on my own,
then dancing but feeling unsettled
these other people with white masks dancing too.

Then in some other place,
could be another time,
I'm at the awful commingling, all the bourgeois
dancing with mannequins and I'm nervous in the middle of it
but give in after a while,
    perverse Lib. Dems. reclining on their scatter cushions
    like nigiri smeared across a tapas dish.

We're all apparatchiks now,
and it's like my whole identity gets mixed up with theirs;
you blast off of the ridge,
the exhaust trailing and—*zzzzzzippp*—
all the sunsets and tanker explosions
and masked others rubbing up against each other...

        Then I'm off out of there
and back home rolling around a bit again
then sleeping
then waking up and
it's the next day four o'clock, only
—wow some guy's there—turn him over and
        he's got one of the white masks from last night on him!

And that's how I got started on this case.

*

The nostalgic future in the Generous Briton in Loughborough at 16.10 on a Thursday; 3am in Cabbage in Sheffield; not readmitted outside Corsica Studios at 21:30;

   feelings of persons present towards one another
   consciousness moves around in the body
   the empty mind
   the power to die consciously
   secondary clear light
   orgastic clarity;

        Woe! The Three Crowns The Mucky Pup!

No drinking outside of social conditions.

      No interpersonal enlightenments,
no creator vision.

A one-way ticket to Sardinia
with the chap there waggling his walking stick up at the mountain
fading into mist or the underside of the clouds
and its one way seemed like a suicide.

To throw off my robot clothes
        to undulate with the endless chain of living forms;

at the hilltop confronted with a view of five counties
the haze over the heather

one's hope in the far-off chance of winning the championship
of actually getting zonked and blotto off drink

losing yourself in love
        so you're there and not there
        released,
striving to serve your abuser.

    At the end of the day the red wine a quick hot passing through.

    Each lift of the nose wheels,
the sandwiches, all little suicides,
        your angry grasp at the expense account
and the fearful importance of work

        apogees of the longed-for erasure;
so pissed you wink out of existence,

the all-day breakfast in the Sidpa Bardo.

*

O [insert name of voyager].
Your mind is indistinct from the horrible things you eat
and the crowding anxiety brought on by your confusing
    ambiguous relations with those around you.
As you drink feel the final clarity escape and, deep inside, the
    growing confounding warmth of empathy.

O [name], as you think about your friends you may become
    frustrated as their empathy lags behind your own.
Fronting up to strangers in a kebab shop
feel the ego both depart from you and crowd in.

Remember:
you're not the only one out boozing tonight:
we flow into and out of one another
like the British on holiday in Tossa de Mar
    [*Habaneras!   the yearning hymns of death*
   Heathrow's carousels a turning masque in the green wood,
       la Habana se llama thanatos],
the fascists in their ecstatic communion.

There flow streams of being-power
through the bar, between and among us
the desperate long only to connect,
subjugate the other within and without—subdue the fear and
    confusion (they will not achieve these aims, the terror only
    grows)
but hopelessly they come together, the voyagers fighting or
    making love
   on waves of care, fleeting and returning.
The momentarily empathetic.
The soft carefulness, reckless liberation.
For three minutes or an hour or for most of the week during our
    trip to Lloret
  or during the World Cup.

O friend,
let the impotent rage wash over you;
it is part of the life flow and an expression
of your unvoiced desire to connect.

O nobly born, listen well:
you are witnessing the magical dance of forms
the mutable wonders of austerity.
Enjoy the dance of the puppets,
they're as much data as you
                       and they dance for you.
Relax upon the caressing bubbles;
Prosecco at the Tory youth conference,
they carry you up and up,
we're buffeted together, ecstatic as we climb.

O friend,
around you stream the wrathful demons of the second bardo;
miners in heavy jackets, skinny cold Argentine soldiers,
these are the products of your imagination;
dead for want of a taxi fare to a work placement,
lost in the Aegean:
    these ego-ghosts of your own creation,
old friends.
Let them wash around you and through you,
know their illusory presence betokens only
your proximity to your ultimate release,
make peace with them, pass along the stream;
your ISA will mature, your REF submission counted,
    your parasitic family will flourish,
      the winter clearance will come
      and the new season after that;

like a trout leaping clear from water
ease yourself into the comfort of empathy,
writhe in the sauce on the plate.

Let your ego wonder like a lost dog in a crowd.

Ten past nine at registration at the opening wine reception at the all welcome wine reception at the plenary with wine and nibbles at the plenary session refreshments provided at lunch on your own at lunch with wine provided for all delegates at lunch sandwiches provided and a pay bar then at the reception after the talk after the final papers after the poetry reading during the poetry reading quickly before the poetry reading instead of the poetry reading at the reception at the dean's town hall wine for all in the pub during the parallel sessions at the MA end of term reading final year exhibition the graduate show the closing reception the final plenary refreshments provided nibbles in the new gallery space with the VC cocktails and canapés with the conference finally over or wine orange juice Kettle Chips sandwiches fruit on sticks Hardy's the warm white wine at the poetry reading the red wine Oyster Bay the biscuits left over from the coffee break it's a quick intimate drink after the Christmas party or a quick one and then what after the supervision it's 19.30 in The Plough and The Horseshoe Inn and the Leather Exchange and the Apple Tree—

        no Catharsis.

   No bust through into the empyrean.

      No illumination.

It ends with you realizing that even the silent beyond has been
   colonised by wankers
      Hesperides amortised
   at the edge of the imagination the machinery of oppression

—it's 5am in La Terrassa on Montjuïc, midnight in premium economy
over the Red Sea or the China Sea,
   it's the afternoon and I'm in the hills above the Wye and I'm high
      as a kite;
   it's the afternoon and I'm wondering what I'll do to fill up my
      evening—

these things will happen;

   it's the end of time in the Senators' Lounge
      it's teatime at Chequers
   it's 04:45 a quickie on the bus
      1905 on the Transandine Express
   1976 Düsseldorf
      Rumi in Napa Valley, one last SoCo and lemonade—
                    last in the sense of last one for this evening
or you want this to be your last or you don't but it is as you'll be
executed after your bottle of Freixenet or euthanized after your
last laps from the bowl old faithful old girl;

      booze is Christ
and his fleshy muscles

           sandwiches.

JOHN LEWIS

At the disappearing point
          as the sun dips at sunset
capital reasserts itself,
     the shadow in the shadows of the shadows

in the midst of the just arrangement
     of labour, the monstrous petit bourgeoise
          the manager at work or at the weekend visiting
          the sacred places, here and Peter Jones;
the libidinal ego relates its exciting object.

At 6am I found myself on Oxford Street,
face already warm from the sun, the air still clear,
bright patches scaling the walls,
     ashes and sparks between.

The glowing orb of the past touched the land and tore the world apart.
And now the glowing orb of the future turns on its axis;
 lights all ways, dispels all shadows.

KUMAR SANGAKKARA

Equinox to equinox and at summer solstice
we turn in ecstasy to the very green god. Green god of water and
   gold,
the quenching draft,
the calming trill in summertime by the sparkling pool in the glade;
gold in the stores at Delphi.

I woke up and it was already the afternoon session (the sun still
   soft that summer),
the game moving on:
        one innings draws to a close
        and the sky changes
the clouds first torn up and then more quickly rolling in.
In the third week of September Pelops-Sangakkara subsides
   beneath the covers.
In late March, in April
        the lost king returns.

1.

You will fail.
Running for the medal
with your last breath stretching towards the line,
    splutter on the sand, you too will recede and pass.

These are some of the specific things that sport can bring to the project:
- beautiful youths sometimes raised up to enormous wealth without regard to their parents' privilege
    - which is better than Oxbridge
        - though the managers are just as monstrous, fingers broken on the rungs
    - though merit is an oppression
- loads of affect
- lots and lots of people from lots of backgrounds all together mostly agreeing at least that this activity they're watching people engaging in is worthwhile
- people acting out the meaningless repetition of work (cf. baseball)
    - miming work, but remember that all work is a miming
- clearer understanding of surplus value
    - Roman Abramovich
    - Hieron I Tyrant of Syracuse
- maybe the opportunities to screw over the prawn cocktail marketing bastards and whatever aristocrats or whichever resource magnates etc. are pyrrhic and they're distractions
    - but at least there's some working through of the habits the victors will need as they take back the newspapers / flush out the vermin
- the parabola
    - you can see it arc and it's almost *only* here so people see it now and again otherwise what is there

25

- and all kinds of other parabolas
- the lines of beauty weaving their charm—and beauty is revolutionary in itself
- youth and beauty
  - though age and all the ways of being are as essential to the project
  - but these things are here really and it's rare that anything's so actual amidst the mummery
- practice breaking their heads
  - though it's chthonic
  - though their violence is there again in ours
- it shows us how obscene official gender is in this place at this time
- exquisite Pherenikos and his numerous advantages
- a woeful depiction of racism in this place at this time
  - in spite of this it is   or it seems to be
    - more diverse than the stock market, academia or publishing, the media, the House of Lords, the bishops and so on
  - it distracts but overall some goodness might come out of this
- show these young women and men their power
- speak back to empire
- clean body, clear mind
- playing golf a couple of times a week should be of some use to the pre-revolutionary body
  - but watching it, or getting too into it, ends up a distraction; the acting out of the dialectic satisfying the instinct for struggle and stifling that which you might call the real impulse
  - but if all of the time you were playing hockey you were always thinking about injustice and riot; consciously comparing your moves and so on
    - or even watching it; thinking of how it's representing work
    - or the dialectic

- or preparing a *coup d'état*
  - consider homosociality the whole time you're at the rugger
  - and it could start right here and it really could—30,000 excited up at Stamford Bridge would be a good place for it to start, tearing up the Fulham Road
- Boris Johnson booed at the Oval in 2018
  - at the cricket, the world's racist game
- maybe there's not fair play just now and that's as it should be
  - no fair play for the rebel tourists or the administrators
  - the level playing fields are at Harrow and Tonbridge
- would prefer to see them diving in the football (which is class war)
  - if you can afford it then let them dive against you
    - the corrupt Yankees beanballing the soon-to-be Streakin' A's [class war] and then going on to the World Series and the next season buying up those busted up players [class war]

2.

I dreamt I read this perfect lost novel, maybe by James Baldwin—
the first half of which was an account of an undergraduate working
to start a collective on campus and use lecture halls for organising.
Then the second half was about Dasein during the revolution;
the characters moving near one another and then past or spinning
past wildly but then finding one another
and the novel was fragmentary in a way that seemed to enact the
utopian tendency of these projects
the structure turning around the point at which the characters
    ceased to articulate
      (ceased to articulate that something which is impossible to achieve
        [an impossibility written into all the accounts, even at the
          beginning])
    but began to live: fulfilled and transcendent,
most persuasively off the page.

The interminable possibility of the test match;
    of the championship stretching before us.
People organising, kind and simple, commingling free from
    oppressors / abusers;
    Villa Diodato without the egos.

The scene with which the text ended had
two people in a room
and another on a telephone talking with one in the room
though the one in the room not on the phone and the one on the
    phone but not in the room were friends
and the one in the room was connecting the other two (one on phone
    one in person),
               a Venn diagram.

And if it had been a book with a telos this would have been it;
 they'd be joined
the fabric of the universe would be rent and these united through their
 intermediary.
But the text ended suddenly and perfectly.

3.

I'd like to take Kumar Sangakkara's dream cover drive for a walk along
    the South Bank
        I'd take his sumptuous cut shot, the sceptre of
            righteousness,
    to a show and after for a drink.

We hadn't him for long;
final autumn sherries, those cuts,
        late flurry of centuries.

And his pull shot!
    Square of the wicket on the off-side.
        Kumar Sangakkara's shots,
    the calming whir of the Super Sopper in summertime;
all the best things about this game.

        Imagine if Sangakkarra came out for the revolution,
Sangakkarra the helmsman,
the mist coming off the dialectic like off a horse in winter.

But probably he won't (and he says he won't)
or if he leads it it'll be some
nationalism or other gimcrack.
        Sangakkara signing off on the room booking as the campus
            goes under.

        I abate.

And your days are numbered too:
    kapos mute through the hiring freezes—you left it too late to
        resist and you
will be washed away;
    Oxford is rubble
                smoke rises from the ruins at Falmer;
ouroboros VCs, your days are numbered
                like the summer passing;
                    last strawberries and cream last Pimm's
    your days are numbered meat-eaters and Evian,

all the worst things about this place;
the pressing maddening grief for the summer that's always ending
    and the grief at the green shoots ever-lessening at Spring, a
    handful less of us at nets
    —your days are numbered the Chelsea Headhunters who
    smashed up Book
Marks, the putrid Alliance of Football Lads—
    I falter with the turning of the seasons
—storm-swift Sangakkara is gone, La Pasionaria finally gone many
    years after the war,
those lost under the flagstones in the middle of things
    swamped by the tide
                sands settle while the kelpy rocks dry.
With her dog the vicar would have seen the still water, sober after the
    passing in the leaf-littered morning.
But she did not come and none will see it;
    none will see the structure fail as the hurricane builds.

Not even the administrators will escape
        not lie retching on the sand the next morning
                            shattered on the bleachéd reefs
desperate fingers losing the masthead
                —no more gallant rearguard at Chelmsford
the tumbling panic of the storm upon us, the tearing flesh and the
    timbers flung
headlong into the silence.

The mud drying now.
He's gone. Chip trays wither on the wind,
grass pressed down in the fields and mud drying under the
    duckboards,
scorecards and blunt pencils trodden into the soil.

DÖNER

Stok Kangri above Leh in the snow
    came to this place it snowed went up on to the pass
        snow deep no road—
    three miles off summit turned back
    continuing to snow
            killed cattle, lived on poor beef without bread or salt.
  the Büyük İskender walks always beside you
on the drop from snowtop

Pea Eye in the brown mantle,
burning through the sticky South West—
on the other side of you the cuckoo clock,
Colin Graves struck down by Azhar Mahmood.
You live on, snow-blind or blinded by the savage sun,
you live on in the spirit of the frantic past.

And, yes, we were wandering who was that twat with you;
    'twas but a dust devil in
Bursa, the home of döners, and thus my home—
Antep, the home of kebabs, and thus my home—
Alder Creek in the lonely Rockies, my home—
Headingley...

    Nameless bureaucrats at the ECB,
stranded at the impassable pass; the impossible past.
Tom Harrison
    feels all the awful pubs of South London
  closed down along with their ghostly clientele.

Who was the other 'droid, who walked with us,
across the broiling sands by the monastery
swirling like snowdrifts around the rupture—
that one always gone
    but still present in the suture
where the bearings meet the flesh,
and flywheel grips tendon

—the snow swirls,
and from the shadows the monster

    that place passed the limits of description and almost of
        imagination
        their long stride along the Nyang Chu valley, Yamdrok lake.

HEADINGLEY CLINAMEN

        Pingu at the crease:
"the universe is in the same state now under strife as was once under
   love":
        the clinamen in Leeds
        that swings about, realigns the great green eye,
        the cold wind that cuts across—

Leeds undid me;
the unvaunted clinamen, left-arm unorthodox,
the long looping lob, the donkey drop
    as in the sky I
  fly my swerving course   underneath the gritty glazing of the
   thundercloud; writing on the heavens;

the cold universe; perfect unchanging sphere: a shoe:
   and on it the seamer's swerve;
     on it the babyless baby; the perfect curveball;
the open doorway—through which the pull shot casts off up out of
   the centrifuge
through the open doorway; a thousand years;
In Padua the grass fine, nibbled short,
   nature's increase,
mind the fairway with soft smooth golfer's soles
as grass fattens lamb—

   all the while the parabola promising a world.

A turn towards
the world of frank intimacy and
   (not quite a free love
         for the world's a world with Beefy in't)
   but to learn to love biding the clinamen
   thoughtful the spit upon the lacquer.

*

Some goodman takes up the stick
      as in the loading bay.
   No forklift, only the externalities of Puritanism,
and this the covenant.

Sacagawea works out a scratch game with a mastodon, hippo,
   asexual lizard, Alfred North Whitehead:

The field is open. If we extend the circle outwards—the centripetal
   boundary,
and the field runs through all points of the universe;
      becomes a quantum, a grand boundary in all directions, from,
         through;

Aaron Finch Belvedere

            darkly striking—

and the rolling boundary is as an organising principle,
that crosses a rope—a sponge—
   and the rolling, tumbling extends across a continent
 gaily chaotic
 grabs the air behind the ball, the air before,
      the air raises the light upon itself—
in your wobble, your shift, the stitches in and out of their orbit,

 at the black cold heart of the kebab.
Of the pitch that extends along and out of everything—
  in the grain of the flesh and in the sparkle of the lacquer,
the new ball swerving

  —large HADRON collider—
 I be the ball on which you're all.

On you,
octopus-handed
   —my extensions,
      we pivot on the air—
above the tiller not for turning;

 sea,
tossed off one time in the back of a boat
in the piccioletta
in the dinghy watching the cricket—
Baraka, Eriugena, Cthulhu a cordon,
 that queer clinamen that lies at the root of order;
  refining itself

amidst the tenthrils;
                the ever-expanding boundary,
    centre and circumference,
the wiggling seamer,
               flung outward from the beginning of things.

ALL THE BLEAK CHIPPIES
for Tom Raworth

Be these sacred places:
    all the Scottish chippies,
the Kinness Fry Bar; KFB in Kennington, Samsun.
Dithyrambos,
    pickle on cabbage.

Urfa Kebab, Köfteci Remzi—all the many chippies
    stirring within.
All the grim chippies.

The round-shouldered fryers.

The leaves stir as the wind rises—
after the apocalypse only a few chip shops left.
    [—*all the awful chip shops;*
        chips at the Oval, chips near Kings Cross
    and in Tunbridge Wells and in Bangor—]
We stepped between the chippies,

        in the world passing out of the world,
    "like tears in the rain," the edifice collapsing.

The wind howls and the demons swarm,

        while you're there forever, compulsively jiggling the
            handle
    on the coffee machine,
that frolic of youth cutting across the whistling wind
        for a second,
        the airbrakes screaming;

all of this will be gone, under new management:
in the dark quiet chippieless night the cyborg shifts in its bed, remembers
Umut 2000, the Fish Dolphin Bar in Sevenoaks, the divine and the dismal as they were
        before the plasma-griffins.
In the starflare how many chip shops, unknown, wink out.

The iron cage is all around us, tightening.

ROOFS

While the cold still slips in
among the banana skins
    and coprolites

cold and hard as any bypass;
the empty trees; the grass flattened,
stones scattered about.

The roof we're under
    —made up from
the satellites
and the lights of the high airliner,

like iron filings,
poles that stretch apart and stay strung together, is
the magnet in which every fragment is magnetised, whole.

*

Steel
retains its heavy
interior.

On the cold pond,
in the ducks, it's frozen.

Smart solemn knowledge of the hatchet,
know the skin coming off the banana,
shut out of the stones'
scent "from

bliss and love
more akin to the emotional life, the viscera,
the central nervous system, which body can only partially express

—bliss and love".

POCAHONTAS
for Neil Young, for William Rowe

What I love best about rivers is:
there's *Dassein* in them.
  To move in and amongst
ever changing and returning—
of the two paths
down one lies
    icy mute piranhas.

And down the other I dreamt
            I was building a wall
which would collapse into the edge of the water.
  Listen to your heart & you will understand.
What flows caress these shores, new & old, speckled
with sand, things cast round the edge of things;
the stranger that lies in the sand-patch, the snowflake,
  while life as experienced is more like waves,
which are silent though something like things.
As if the Earth were just a dead thing you could claim:
the trackless forest,
the great many-linked train that heaves with the unbinding of
    continents.

  Remain—
within the thronging strangeness
of things
  reverberate all through & among one another.
Mankind and the blade of grass.

LAURA BRANIGAN

"Nothing abides:
>the river stops, the sun sets,
>living is dying, the mountains melt into the valleys,
>the zodiac is but a revolution

>>—in all of this am I to prove the one stable thing?"

1.

Piano, piano,

>I wake up sweating, cut down from the column;
from the fleshy coil revolving.

AOI!
>The song that remains,

for those suddenly dead after long misery:
>expired under a stone;
>assassinated while on trial for corruption in Valencia—
>>who died unnecessarily under homeopathy;
>for the billion lambs upon the spit;
>the cricketers who killed themselves;
>those who accidentally got out the wrong side of an old train
>>into the path of another train;
>or thought they saw a ghost of their future self and jumped out
>>between stations;

>   or feared exposure and hanged themselves;
>   or died alone   —
> *AOI!* The deserving dead!
>   Blown to bits in the Challenger disaster, all alone even
>   together;
>   locked in an oven in the fibre glass factory;
>   faithless street dogs frozen;
>   down, down from a roof after tinkering with an aerial.

> Those inside and just outside of things, best wishes for your
>   journey!

>   On this side
>   I hear only scuffling:
> John Muir's nature sliding under the crust and into the mud—

>   *AOI!*

As if events were knowable!

>   If I started shouting out
>   would she hear me, up beyond the cloudy massif,
>   behind the steam train on its grand curve,
>   high among the orders of the angels?
>   And if she did
>   and turned that practised and perfect organ
>   towards me,
>   you know, I think that I should simply shrivel
>   —a tiny portion of a person,
>   a bee upon the breeze.

2.

Laura Branigan's voice is
handsome and impossible:

> as wide as the pampas
> as mad as Bayreuth;

> two kinds of emptiness:
> the echoing emptiness in the underpass;
> the hollowness of all things.

As fitting as a church in the countryside,
water without a desert—
whether from work or straight out of bed,
from the steps of an altar
                —dynamite,

> terrible in its power.

> The low horizon and the damp under;
> the blue in the sky and, higher, the frost;
> the nimbus-piercing mountaintops and the grumbling yeti
> (the mountain promises unending ascent while the monsters
>   lament
>   behind the unreachable ridge);
> the lovely uramaki, the terrible wasabi.

She was a manhole cover—
    the Exocet of unconstraint

the voice, the bridge and tunnel, down like a rock: the arena, the
   stone mind
      and the superego
   never stopping not considering and always considering

Laura Branigan posits the breathless ego soaring
while yet she performs the bitter bounds of control.

3.

Long Island Sound.
A quiet sandwich on the promenade,
   clouds on the horizon.
     Walt Whitman's beard forms
        and Laura's face above, smiling as in a dream—

before, like all clouds, she's gone.

   Beauty lead us to sympathy;
at the turn of the stair
   softly, like the circling swift,
   the loud but secretive wren
         in its bubbling absence
   flies above the wind but cannot rise.

The late triumphs at Viña del Mar,
   feeling a little softer

but in the evening on the recliner
   the divided world fades,
   the shock of loving mellowed,
     the cool Pacific,
   marine layer rolling in
      as the seaborn laser show comes into view,
      one last time.

Bee wavering towards the hive;
the autumn coming and the work done,

I'm a bee buzzing home to die,
the queen ready in her cage for winter.

The Sound, the sandwich, the bee:
all wait for the right voices.

WORK IN SPACE
for Jennifer Cooke

This one time I got a job on Io
    or out by Aldebaran
stacking power couplings,
    the second week I arrived late all five days and they fired me.

In other far parts of the galaxy casually employed and let go,
    "working / not working."

When you have a job in space you will still have to turn up on time.
Even when you have a job in space you will still have to turn up on time;
    set your alarm, move around or under the cosmic city.

Your work will be—walking on the ceiling in Velcro shoes—
    ontologically aligned with capital.

*

On past the coral shores, the
lifeguard up atop the marvellous ladder, on patrol on Planet Splash.
One time I had to administer the intravenous translation at the space
    commission
    once selling Han Solo jackets
opening the pod bay doors for 8 hours a day—

    the wild flower 'neath the shepherd's foot,
an unlicensed junk freighter, Lymeswold.
Indicator ticking in the gyratory.

*

The far future alien considering human consciousness,
the ghastly imposition of the working week.

Cambozola. Trainees on the satellite.
In the mist the holobooth glowing.

Got work scooping the slippery avocado balls—
couldn't hold them and I lost it, replaced by David, the betentacled
   squid.

*

The tachograph will still turn,
        an arsehole will monitor you, will line-manage you.

        All our works pass out beyond the ends of the blocked-out work
    week. All the jobs end. All of us working
but as yet untranslated,
staring back down the ultrasound—
pumping gas on the Outer Rim.

In the dark heart of the bureaucratic city the museum of work-
   placements.
In the cold heart of the universal city the middle managers' Hall of
   Fame,
the Coruscant precariat.

*

My work is to move around the galaxy understanding.
To share in the knowledge of others,
                to become like others,
to mix minds with strangers, with strange beings from across the universe
to know all and to have all know me.

Beyond the stars the bourgeois understanding of work might not apply,
between the cold gears of the universe
the little meaning you find in labour might melt away,
become an idleness not consumption.

You still might get that internship in Terabithia.
Could finally get a job with a stationery cupboard, order up Post-Its.
My job was to answer the phone and catch sudden glimpses of myself in the office
    door swinging open, a flash on the glass of the desk.

*

I drove a space taxi but since the last people were cut out of the driver-market
I'm no longer economically productive or necessary;
not as producer nor soldier,
so I am cast aside and I am killed.

I am the algorithm and you will never understand my machinery;
      my Oxbridge mankads.

I would be fucked in a meritocracy
anyone reading this would be fucked in a meritocracy.
Almost everyone.
The seven jealousies:
Keston, Jacob Rees-Mogg; the virtuous meritocrats.

*

A space whaleman.
My peg leg my glass eye my cyborg protuberance my golden eyebrow
the eternal authenticities of work and self-sacrifice, no
    bourgeois bohemians in space, no
        cricket administrators:
those who would make the just and perfect unjust.

In space no zero hours.
No fascist English majority.
There will be no inhouse wellness coaching.
In space no one will listen to you read—
lyric space; the long, loud, bright ring of infinity;
    tinnitus, the ion engines.

Syntax vectors among phosgene balloons
in the sparky dark of the emperor's smithies.
Three weeks' training programme at a protein recycling combine.
We will all retire, then one day there'll be a world where even the
    computers won't
    have to work,
service bots put out to pasture.

Boiling freezing sunset on Ganymede,
>	on Ganymede the associate lecturer at 1am; second
>	marking—
>on Ganymede the grass soft, the loam, the putting green, breath
>fogs the
windshield, the ice-miner fallen from the airlock—
external examiner flames out above Calypso.

*

Listen!

>Sky crack, cosmic thunder;
>trumpets below the turning bottom of the galactic city—

>>spectral dolphins jagging
>along the vibrating boundary—
>>cosmos expands,
>>>blood from the fountains;
>>>speckles the creamy marble and the arching orca
>>>>the breaching humpback.

>The cosmopolitan city

dispersed across the galaxy;
>not one will need receipt for travel expenses

>not one flung out from the burnished city
>will be finally hired.

>The cage tightening.

Know you the great city;
>among the distant rings the spangled city.

TWO PATHS

I came to a division;
    Along the grassy turn to the left
    leaf-logged and dewy-grassed and mulched
    between fosse and path danced black monsters
    you might see move like steel firing, bellows through the ribcage
    as, icy, the creatures 'clean clear minds
    they knew knowing between the vines
    over dockleaf and cowslip.

    While to the right, a clearing before a pond
    and in the trees
                    interstellar entropy.
    On one path white frozen clouds
    and rolling grey, with swatches of that rimey blue—
    above the other conjecturally you see the stars spin,
    flash or pop.

    I needn't state the path I trod,
    or my head thick and buzzing against the molten gale,
    that one might fall out of life and into the autonomous.
    Blackness upon blackness.

*

    What glistens at the heart of the axe head?
    What darkness in the rock belly?
    In the old radio
    under brittle insulation
    the dull shine, deep within the wire.

THE A1

        A thousand years ago!

...the train before
and behind,   out beyond the defile,
  soft feet on sand,
     cinches scraping.

    At evening, the cat knelt by a fire at the centre of the oasis, paw
       on glinting hilt:
  "o how do I fucking hate thee sand, in my paws, in my greasy ear
    folds,
    hate life alone on the road but ever pushing onwards—long live
      leaving."

Mexico is thanatos—
   the jungle rustling against the speeder;
        "if the buzzing jungle speaks its soul to you
if your cock drops off from ayahuasca,
   you will have reached your destination."

The service station at Markham Moor, the white light that is allness.

Way down south, "between death and life—
   to York, to Alnwick—
we moved, as all lovers move."

*

Lorry drivers. If return were possible, what might we have carried
south, into the cabaret of destruction?
A manifest: string beans, cheese—in the lost world, the old right
world—records.
    But in the broken world:
almond croissants to Patisserie Valerie (arena of death); the grand
mechanism of love; all the attempts to love differently; fennel;
we carried the irrefutable fact that this loving doesn't work; light
loofah; mattresses; heavy were the manifold accoutrements of
love; ginger, normal vegetables.

When you have learnt to love while relinquishing control,
when you affirm the comingling bodies in collaborative jouissance—
    in loving kindness in the multi-faith prayer room—

my self working, my self loving
    on the sand, the softened sound, breeze and a flash on the water,
        in Odessa,
in the service station, feeling the paradigm around us.

This, then, was the junction for Burning Man;
this the seat of our loving.
    In the gelid rock pools and up scrubby escarpment the
cannibal geckoes fucking in the open. The blank world their quiet
bower,
while a silent meteor flares overhead, a rocket exploding.

*

Rich England, sheep-clipped tilth right up the A1.
The last drop of the morning's cloudburst
    off of the windscreen as the dashboard twinkled.
  The Services approached;
    clear clean generous joy in loving and in its careless receiving,
the moments immediately preceding the first morning of the first
    test match of the summer, the brassy knell of love, parked up at
    the Little Chef:
        the first morning of the first test match of the summer in
           perpetuity.

An unteleological love and its return, "a more mutual lying together."
On the sunlit uplands, the service station, the dogging circle—or a
    freedom that's not had the patriarchy stitched into it;
    everyone bundled together on the uterine beach;

astronauts on the International Space Station, registered
    Republicans, having their minds blown, falling in love at 17,150
    miles per hour;
    like in a murder mystery, as in a romcom.

The sunlit uplands, the glowing A-1 passed through in a cutting;
    into the gathering shade at evening
        as the fields lost their colour beside the still roaring dell:
                Hatfield: thanatos, Welwyn Garden City: thanatos, Stevenage: thanatos, Baldock: thanatos, Letchworth Garden City: thanatos, Huntingdon: thanatos, Peterborough: thanatos, Grantham: thanatos, Newark-on-Trent: thanatos, Retford: thanatos, Doncaster: thanatos, Leeds: thanatos, Harrogate: thanatos, York: thanatos, Ripon: thanatos, Darlington: thanatos, Durham: thanatos, Gateshead: thanatos, Newcastle: thanatos, Alnwick: thanatos, and Berwick: thanatos.

    Cold aurochs in the layby, Emil Bergson on the prairie for one
        reason and
Alexandra there to die, also. The Great Plains: an orgiastic futurity,
the mountains of Mexico: utopian congresses.

    Coupling on the hillocks, at Zabriskie Point—

Emil's eros a thanatos, this natural and abundant gift,
the universal life force,
    without design or purpose.

*

The last session of the last test:
    you will have reached and you will have fallen short.

Upon leaving
those things which you had intended to discover will have become
    obscured;
        your desires, as you near your destination
            (the charnel house within),
    live among the creatures of the night
        in the oasis of hypnagogia;
    the dream-like purgatory of our customary relations, the
        penetrating key upon the supplicating lock.

Relations without epiphanies!

*

It's 02:30 and PCs Barry and Keith are on the road between
   Retford and Newark-on-Trent,
sad and sweet from loving without coercion.
   Or,
says Keith,
   those who would love generously and without discrimination.

The lonely drivers:
plummy horse transporter,
one carrying iguanas to the safari park,
one with mattresses (bound for what pinched ecstasies! how
   many death rattles!).
In the squad car both are lonely;
the private ambulance carrying the dead,
loose llamas on the hard shoulder;

I'm a French teacher on the road near Ripon,
I am glad—at the end of the day—that my desire is bounded.

On the A1 I'm
the guy with the lizards, thinking about how he'd seen growing up
   as accumulation—
not counted on
losing bits of yourself that won't be there for the next blunder
      I wish I'd done this or that,
he thinks,
      but I've never been less than I am now
—dropping back from the peloton and out of sight.

Mattress driver as the lorry tips:
   at last,
   the end of the evacuated life!

Just like hot-desking is unequivocally an oppression.
Welwyn to Letchworth. No sex is communal, a lonely passing
 through, "the Term between".

  Somewhere near the road
  the police equine trainer moved from one room into another to
    find you stretched out on the bed—all body and person.

  One, driving, sees the relentless ordering of life about desire
  run slowly dry—
    hard to know who could think that there could be a utopian
      love-making.

  Though one, up on the wind turbine,
    remains so sure,
  the high airs still delight.

*

All the animals around the A1
will be connected as if by an airy net,
as if the ponies humping in the fields will become
a thingful beingness in the open.

Count Elmo Mancini tumbles in his Ferrari:

  ah the flapping flesh
    Felicità
  o the clacking bones
    Felicità   felicità
  a phone call you weren't expecting / a glass of wine and a sandwich
    /
  our simple coitus /

a pizza in the moonlight by the piazza /
   a conception on holiday /
   the red glare of Betelgeuse,
       Antares upon our glistening backs—

could we learn it of the Green World?—
Love outside the hierarchy?

           The sacred mingling at the cocktail party
   administered by the wondrous goddess,
   the seasons will turn the vegetables in the fields,

               rise up and fall back,
fingers around the balled-up soul
     will bring up marrows from the seed,
throw up nourishing radishes,
     rhizomes from love's wild garden
   from the undifferentiated flow and slither
           of a love unmanaged before the lowing milkers.

The continuous future of the animate natural world:
love in the literal and figurative darkness
   each dark to the others

               Thelma and Louise

though the loving continues

    like lights flickering on and off across the city—
        beginning and quickly / less quickly finishing,

from the police helicopter,

        leaving *Viva Las Vegas*,
satnav (the traces of the tracks) at the closing off of the prairie
erotothanatos

& in the orgasmic super-freedom of the plain
                the blue skies—

Mr. Casaubon in the Vatican,

      the distant dusty tracks
    small footsteps already half-erased

              my love alone at the edge of the world.

ODE TO DOGS

I am the moon

BRING UP BETHLEHEM

This is my dream:

I'm in abstract passing over the city
my perspective is unclear
    from the forests in the hills
over the suburbs that look down on the centre
up and down the old streets
    and as in a vision I see society laid out
        the president a cat (stupid like a cat) atoy with the ministers.

In the still woods
winter in summer, faint mist and crow calls
sun cooler under the leaves

the city splendid like a dream
faint traces in the mulch
light lines in the trees,
while the long march down from the pass
    is over in an instant
grass waves where it's not yet trodden down around God's righteous
    roundabout—

we sorted out the snacks for the cabildo
we arranged the soft drinks for the cabildo
and from the forests the multitude
between the trees the mobile cabildo
between the trees skipping flames
Sean was there a flame among the branches
Sean was there his voice clear at the cabildo.

I imagined myself at the Plaza de la Dignidad,
    imagined myself at the cabildo
the disgraced ex-minister there
the poet Ho Chi Minh
    all the ambivalent remittances of poetry

  —craft so long to learn,
  life so short

while at the other end of the city
the hysterical cops were throwing a man down the vent of the metro
    where he got electrocuted and died
from the forest trickles dignity

Chanticleer was at the cabildo—*kokoroko*!
while the cops burnt the trees
and the city burning all over tonight
smash our way into JD Sports and have our cabildo there
      —the loud sweet sound!—
cops burnt down the cinema
the university the Violeta Parra museum
their own cop church
opened up torture chambers in the metro
  burnt down the stations, the bones still beneath from last time
gassed me at work and at home
I was on my way to give a lecture on *The Border Trilogy*
going to that screening of *Meek's Cutoff*
I was on my way to a seminar on Frederic Remington's late paintings
a class on Andy Warhol's *Lonesome Cowboys*
Ishmael Reed's *Yellow Back Radio Broke-Down*
the "New Mexico Poem" of Diane di Prima
Bad Day at Black Rock, *Cogewea*,
Captain Apache—

and in the forests and in the canyons
above below the city
the trumpets ring and

> "the third day broke, bleak and windy. At sunrise the Ents' voices rose to a great clamour and then died down again. As the morning wore on the wind fell and the air grew heavy with expectancy. The hobbits could see that Quickbeam was now listening intently, although to them, down in the dell of his ent-house, the sound of the Moot was faint."

ODE AT THE BEGINNING OF THE UNIVERSE

    A pinhole
         the world sucked out of the world
into the core of a star cluster—

    space just a space which is emptiness
    cosmos a space in a particular position, real estate;
  all the sound sucked out of the world—

then the soft light flicking out

              nothing

but after a short pause a long pause you can't tell
    glowing behind the scenery
  cream and off-white then bright white magnesium white
        blinding and rainbow

everything expanding

              vanilla coral ivory lace Olympic sonic white
  morning light frosted dawn absolute white moon shimmer fine
    cream cream tea orchid white
  white silver snow day white dove
pure white no it's not it's a rainbow in it with everything in it a snow
  leopard, a
  world full of colours,
            all white on the night,
    trumpeting the party horns!
    streamers tumbling!
    cosmic Byzantium, ghostly outlines behind all things,

                    shines out
                the future city rises
                    four towers
                    great encircling cycle lanes
                            the sparkling stars fall into alignment
stormtroopers killed by the celebrating crowd outside the Senate
penguins take the tracking station
                            the endless empire of peace commences

            universe's
                        gala.

ACKNOWLEDGEMENTS

Thanks to Jennifer Cooke and Jeff Hilson, who read this book before its submission, and Tim Atkins, who read the poems as they were written.

A version of 'Ode at the End of the World' appeared in a pamphlet prepared for a reading by Edward Gonzalez at the Pontificia Universidad Católica de Chile (2018).

A version of 'Pocahontas' appeared in *Veer Journal 4 – Veer Vier: For Will Rowe* (2014).

Versions of 'Mending Wall' and 'Two Paths' appeared in *Poetry Wales* (2014).

A version of 'Döner' appeared as a broadside published by Michael Kindellan at the University of Sheffield (2015).

A version of 'The A1' appeared in *Erotoplasty* (2018).

'Norte Sur,' a free Spanish translation by Macarena Urzúa Opazo and Jèssica Pujol Duran of a version of 'The A1,' appeared on *Vallejo & Co* (2018) and in *Antología bilingüe Po-Ex* (2018).

'N2,' a free Catalan translation by Jèssica Pujol Duran of a version of 'The A1,' appeared on *Vallejo & Co.* (2018) and in the *Llengües de foc* anthology (2020).

A version of 'Laura Branigan' appeared in *Erotoplasty* (2020).

A version of 'Work in Space' appeared in *Wretched Strangers*, Boiler House Press (2018).

A version of 'All the Bleak Chippies' won first prize, adults category, in the 2018 Ledbury Poetry Festival Poetry Competition.

A version of 'Headingley Clinamen' was published in an anthology of work from the Facultad de Letras of the Pontificia Universidad Católica de Chile (2021).

A version of 'Bring up Bethlehem' was published in *Corroding the Now*, Crater Press (2021).

There's a lot of collage in these poems, which incorporate words by many other writers. Texts that are quoted from or paraphrased repeatedly and/or prominently include Ralph Metzner and Timothy Leary's *The Psychedelic Experience*, *The Cantos of Ezra Pound*, *Star Wars*, George Eliot's *Middlemarch*, *A1: Britain's Longest Road*, *Silent Running*, *Cool Runnings*, *2001: A Space Odyssey*, Samuel R. Delany's *Trouble on Triton* and *Dhalgren*, Emily Witt's *Future Sex*, *The Song Remains the Same*, *Aliens*, *Blade Runner*, Larry McMurtry's *Lonesome Dove*, Charles Olson's *The Maximus Poems*, *Woodstock*, Rainer Maria Rilke's *Duino Elegies*, Herman Melville's *Mardi, and a Voyage Thither* and Willa Cather's *O Pioneers!*

Space Odes
By R. T. A. Parker

First published in this edition by Boiler House Press, 2021
Part of UEA Publishing Project
All rights reserved
© R. T. A. Parker, 2021

The right of R. T. A. Parker to be identified as the author of this work has been asserted in accordance with the Copyright, Design & Patents Act, 1988.

Design and typesetting by Emily Benton Book Design
emilybentonbookdesigner.co.uk

Typeset in Arnhem
Printed by Imprint Digital, UK
Distributed by NBN International

This book is sold subject to the condition that it shall not, by way of trade or otherwise, be lent, resold, hired out, stored in a retrieval system, or otherwise circulated without the publisher's prior consent in any form of binding or cover other than that in which it is published and without a similar condition including this condition being imposed on the subsequent purchaser.

ISBN 978-1-913861-34-6